MESSAGE FOR THE SISTERS

By

Russell Russell

Table of Contents

Introduction 4

Chapter 1
New World Destructive Order...5

Chapter 2
University Information Destructive Order..7

Chapter 3
Business 13

Chapter 4
Christian and Islam Context... 15

Chapter 5
Soul 23

Chapter 6
Links to God and Satan 26

Chapter 7
Algorithms 52

Chapter 8
How to kill a lot of HUMANS 61

Chapter 9
Calculation Collective 65

Chapter 10
Bye, Bye, not Buy Buy! 69

Introduction

This book contains a message for Christian and Muslim women.

What you read here I bear witness to by my spirit – that there is a destructive order upon this earth that acts against God and God's creation.

Chapter 1

New World Destructive Order

Whatever you believe your essence to be: The New World Destructive Order is driven to kill it. Like a preprogramed algorithm riding a missile through the sky it seeks to destroy the biological life forms and the human essence.

The economic machine rules the Earth driven by oil and coal; it leaves gas in the atmosphere that traps sunlight and causes warming, that in turn shifts weather patterns altering natural environments and killing species that do not have time to adapt.

The United Nations promised to protect us. Over the last 50 years we have become an economic robot; making goods, consuming natural habitat, and depleting our humanity as we pass time to pay bills, over-eat, becoming addicted to legal and illegal drugs, alcohol, porn, wars and shopping.

Humans are emotional individuals and not reliant upon reflection upon species. We think and feel about other humans with love and care seeking meaning to life.

However, we have been told by scientists we are now undergoing a 'biological annihilation' and species are under threat: this must have some affect upon us. If not we cannot be said to care about animals and nature.

So do we care? I mean do you care if one million species of plant, insect, and animals die forever?

They will if climate change continues at the present pace.

Then what?

How about millions in developing countries starving and being flooded out of their homes?

All because of what?

A continuing way of life fuelled by coal and oil. A **destructive order** led by a minority of leaders across the planet and their systems of control.

Welcome to the NEW WORLD DESTRUCTIVE ORDER

Chapter 2

University Information Destructive Order

Understood to religious logic: God gave life via a biological system that unfolded. We experience its creation and know facts it has existed (according to science) from bacteria, insect, plant, dinosaurs, trees, fish, elephants, sub humans, modern humans and so forth.

New World Destructive Order has a conglomerate of information probability fields acting through people and systemic institutions of thought that act to attack the God given biological process as upheld in all species of plant, insect, animal, human life forms.

The conglomerate of information needed to sustain the overall destructive system is inherently produced within the university system. Here we get great research and invention which the business world uses.

Pharmaceuticals: drugs proscribed to us. Engineering; cars, planes, buildings. Technology: computers, atomic missile systems, internet. Written articulated laws that allow big business to avoid paying correct tax. And all number of specialized degrees for any subject matter that exists. These highly educated creative knowledgeable people go on to join big business and direct the world order especially through politics and media.

Google is responsible for more advertising to buy goods than any other medium. The modern day outcome is more greenhouse gas emissions as people are programmed to keep buying goods. Control of the information structure via algorithms. The algorithms can favour certain companies that pay for ads and hence influence minds.

The economic reality is one based around advertising so we cannot accuse anyone they should not advertise or supply modern ways how and who to advertise to. However it has to be said that this phenomenal rise is a part of the probability of the destructive order.

There isn't a bunch of people in communication conspiring to cause destruction, but there are entities spread across all mediums involving people, where we can show where there is evidence of destructive output. And which when linked to other frames of reference show them each to be part of the destructive order.

This order is one of probability or chance of occurrence or likelihood to cause destruction, where we can state that each component, be it framed as political-media-business-university output: Acts as an overall influence to set the world up for a decent chance of biological species destruction.

In short: the university educated get jobs in business that in turn is responsible for habitat destruction and pollution. Politicians allow these activities to occur without introducing protective laws and the media do not report the exploitation. Left for 50 years we get today's climate emergency, systemic racism, obesity epidemic, Covid-19 spread across the world, trillions dollars of debt, and migrants floating across the sea where some of them drown or get penned in at a migrant camp.

We live within governments' dictate spurned on by what the media decide to report or not report to us. There is so much nefarious activity going on like tax avoidance, international pollution, wars; we don't get to hear about most of these activities, let alone find out the reasons around who is supporting factions with guns and bombs. People, like in Yemen and Syria, are left to the mercy of war lords, where some literally starve to death, or get blown up by a bomb.

13 million are at risk of starvation, in Yemen according to the UN.

Civil war in Syria has left more than 400,000 people dead.

Be clear, educated people create bomb technology, educated people give the orders to drop them or supply them, international businesses employs as many highly educated informed specialists it can and has too. They set across the earth striking business deals, enforcing trade, transport, financial debt loan structures, and from their spoils we get jobs and contribute via taxes to the political societal system. Sure the positives outweigh the negatives but the end result is a destructive threat to the human race: climate change.

Had these 4 key components (political-media-business-university) unfolded with better sense to protect the human race and with more duty of care they would have not allowed and encouraged environmental damage via fossil fuel exploitation (at the cost of species, ecology, and food chain stability) and nor would they have continued mass starvation of millions of people per year from Africa and Asia.

Had every big billionaire company placed their cheated tax funds to feed the starving over the last 10 years they would have saved the lives of 100 million people. Instead of that they continue to insist we keep buying more and more: because logically there are more profits to be made in a world economy of more and more. Which allows more power and influence to these small groups of people, who in business are now running an algorithm racket spread across the internet; that allows super-surveillance-intelligence-gathering information to be collected and used to manipulate humans to buy products.

This expanding ability to corrupt the human mind into a buy goods state of mind, at any cost to the environment, has with it all sorts of surrounding and emergent influences where we can argue this course is corruption of the human spirit or soul or essence – whatever you use by definition – what is deemed the most valuable part of a person and is stated as being eternal by most religions.

Understood without religious frame of reference you would call it a reflection of your most treasured human values that you hold emotionally, intelligently with feeling and care. Where you may not believe in an eternal outcome, but where you will believe humans are all linked from one generation to the next, and where we have some duty held in our consciences to protect the planet and protect the chances of other human populations to exist in the future. You may not reflect over this but if asked would concur.

Once humans begin to stray from that deeply felt unspoken principle of: protecting life as we know it, there would be some problem. That problem would show evidence that we have drifted from that principle. That evidence is climate change.

There cannot be that much evidence shown within your personal life that you are forgetting about protection and care. I mean what individual is that much different to the next? We all mean well and hope for the best for ourselves and most others. We do not mean bad or poor outcomes. We love and show humour and kindness to others. Sure some are experts at care: like a mother and baby, or a loving couple at marriage, kindness to a beggar in the street… we all possess a caring nature albeit some people achieve more with these abilities.

So the essence as shown in our personal lives is protected. But as an output as a collective of billions of us we are contradicting our morality and spirituality because we are draining the environment from what it can give at a rate higher than it can replenish itself with trees, fresh air, water, and ultimately food.

We seem crazed on objects, money, jobs, fashion and holidays and entertainment. Only then would we consider animal species, trees, plants and insects that we take for granted. This stuff held as a scientifically stated problem is an information content, something we can reflect upon. It is not natural to us that we have to think about such a large concern and problem that it be judged by our soul.

So it is very difficult to solve the problem based upon force of our habits having been constructed via previous generations where they never had to regard the human race and its overall direction around environment and natural resources. We just took what we wanted as and when we wanted it. That is more or less what society has been allowed to do by governments worldwide.

As we try to come to terms with our predicament I am merely stating that the likes of business; is trying to get us to buy more via billions of dollars in adverts suggesting to our minds buy-buy-buy. Yes, but remember the opposing message – CO_2, CO_2, CO_2, equals death to species, and hence biological diversity death, where coincidently our chances of a quality civilized life where we have time to think and feel and make moral intelligent decisions is depleted. And where we find ourselves having to decide to what level of protection do we wish to offer the environment.

Unless we decide what protection to offer and then implement it; we will drift and be at the mercy and influence of the political order, media order, university order, business order **New World Destructive Order.**

Chapter 3

Business

Consumerism has been the key idea for society for decades, it paved way to pay for everything we see around us. Money does make the world go around, people need jobs and stuff to exchange and this we might call the basic principles of economy.

Meanwhile, world governments chose to ignore pollution and natural environmental loses. And from the 1980's we put more greenhouse gases into the air than the total since humans begun to exist.

The UN got us to avoid another world war, but they let the environment down and let emissions from oil and coal create what today is called climate change.

The scientific warnings for climate change were ignored from the media and so we swept into this millennia without any collective knowledge about the dangers. The media simply did not educate us. And so, like economic sheep, we continued along the consumerism idea with its global companies and big tax free profits.

Politicians continued to burn coal and today we find that we have lost a lot of natural habitat and are on course to hit a climate change target that will wipe out the coral reef, 40% species, and a billion people to starve next century.

During our time politicians have followed a trillion dollar debt society where governments keep taking loans from those with money and spending it on arms, roads, hospitals and other modern structural needs that aim to benefit a countries people. These loans have interest and because of this, it can be argued we lose roads, houses, education, hospitals, and other structural needs. Hard to gauge, but we can be certain that the richest country in the world (USA) has a massive homeless problem indicating money was not spent on cheap rental social housing. Meanwhile in the UK there is a child hunger problem. Is this a joke?

All the different compartments of business, energy supply, media, and political economic theory have modernized the world as we know it with its colossal inventiveness. The down side is climate change caused by fossil fuels, and habitat destruction caused by city and road building. The knock on effect is more floods, fires, species decline, human migration, starvation, and a 7 trillion dollar loss to economy by 2050, which means less hospitals and healthcare and more deaths.

Chapter 4

Christian and Islam Context

The **New World Destructive Order** is a fast managing economic system that manufactures a structure of societal reality that attempts to destabilize the biological system. Understood in Christian biblical terms is an affront to God's biological system by what they call Satan which is defined as an overall counter system to God.

This so called **Satanic** system is an out of date old fashioned name that understood in modern parlance is simply a set of unified acting probability fields that undermine the very life process held in the biological system. This includes the altering consciousness found in humans.

Meanwhile spiritual religious understanding is a system that acts to defend the biological system via ideas and insights around virtue; especially warnings around the destructive qualities – greed, hate, selfishness. Whilst encouraging kindness, love, care, lack of greed as guiding principles for human awareness. This awareness to such themes is what can be named as awareness of the soul. Some people lose this awareness or leave it shallow. Replacing that awareness with what?

Religious books and practices are an information system about God normally via the conduit of a human. This information presented to us is a communication telling us about vital qualities needed to uphold the defence of life. Its key idea is virtue that transfers to a better now and afterlife with respect and love for life. This advice is a contract between the information state that is of God. Or given another understanding, is God.

The interaction at this level is the human free will and awareness acting with God for God and creation of life forms.

The constructive order is life giving information creation via biological system producing outcomes. If the biological system can be destroyed by dark force system then human life fails.

The **New World Destructive Order** relies upon the probability where for IT (if IT were conscious as Christianity implies) we would call it hope and strategy to destroy all life forms by atomic weapons or biological disorders that act as weapons (like COVID 19) or algorithm weapons (used on the internet) or climate change. These four weapon systems are its current method to succeed. Its best chance to succeed. And would rely upon each weapon being utilized by groups of dominating humans, who employ the highly educated as a supporting mechanism to uphold a collective thought process that outputs destructive outcomes.

Political orders and big international business structures are potential agencies to create effective attacks via pollution, climate change, war, continual advertising via algorithms on systems like Google that encourage continually the buying of products like a process in time;

that indirectly causes CO2 emissions and climate change, which then causes biological attack upon soil, decline of insect, plant, animal and eventually human species.

Such outcomes do not need to be consciously arrived at. The very structure of the probabilities, interwoven within reality have a natural hidden action that will shift towards the attack of a biological system or system that serves that biology.

So – in the case of humans we have to fight off obesity, pollution, accidents, ecological breakdown, floods fires, and other natural phenomena like Covid-19 that can kill. If we are in a God / light frame of probability our chances of success to maintain life equilibrium is likely. If the dark frame, unlikely.

Yes, we are in a mixed flux of life death, growth decline mixed outcomes. Life is pitted within dualities. But when life is sliding into extinction as currently is occurring through climate change, or where bombs in your society force you to live in a war zone, this is New World Destructive Order.

Probability structures are everywhere and unfold together in displaced settings. Hence we can see society and human culture as an ever growing system of unpredicted changes mixed with designed foreseen probable changes. As humans we like to be able to predict, but who 200 years ago would have known of rockets, cars, computers, atom bombs and television sets?

Limitations of prediction fall to natural outcomes. We move, create and see what comes with some planning. We do not rely solely on prediction and the certainties of proofs. We forge ahead with risks accompanying us.

Satan or dark force is a probability of destruction opposing the probability light force or God. Depending on the vocabulary you are used to framing things in.

Light force is a probability construction. This is a design program to sustain and produce life. Its goal and outcome is sustainable life.

Where the so called human soul has as a key component of what it is: an agreement and instruction by God to uphold as a work force a part of a collective where we sustain the principle of LIFE and oppose the principle and probability of Death and Dark force destruction.

Look at any example of life, like for instance babies and joy of family and friends compared to death disease and bombs.

Within the human collective some groups become devoid of any respectable ability to enjoy life or sustain life to its full or decent degrees. People in war zones live in fear with declining qualities of positive emotions and positive experiences because others are attacking and killing, so they have to defend their country with equal emotional life shattering violence. Such is the probability that is the New World Destructive Order.

A different type of killing exists that we can call naturally accidental. Others might drive a car and kill a person by the probability that is defined as a destructive life taking element; not of conscious will but lack of skill to overcome the existing chance of failure, via accident, that naturally exists within reality.

Accidents and destruction occur like plane crashes, or broken legs in sport because there is a chance of them occurring. Reality as we know it holds these chances. Experience and observation proves this. We could frame this as saying that if the information we are in or what surrounds us is structured in a way that is very unfavourable we are likely to meet a bad outcome.

Equally here, in what is being stated and framed in a modern explanation, climate change is a structure of information or if you prefer – circumstances that we are caught within as an 8 billion human collective. It is a very unfavourable set of circumstances and understood simply is a method of attack to destroy biological life forms.

As heat increases species will die out including 99% of the coral reef around 2 Celsius degrees. For every degree more than now we lose up to 10% of the crop yields which impacts on the poorest of people especially those starving and hungry already; this is very-very serious in regards to starvation of millions to billions of people potentially.

So understood to the frame we currently use around God; it is more logical to state: that key probability information from God once ignored, as it is being ignored in relation to climate change and the best biological suited temperature of 1.5 degrees, we are partaking in destruction of life species process and thus attacking the biological system that creates life. This is the situation held as a spiritual understanding and everyday problem for this current near population of 8 billion people.

God as an information state (or if you are Buddhist or atheist you would call it reality) sends information by myriad methods to all life forms where within all actions of each life form is an optimum route to take, surrounded by less optimum choices where that life form has a chance to survive or destroy itself and its own habitat and species type be it early, or now, or later.

In my opinion all outcomes are held in probabilities long before they occur. You then have a chance, given the turning of time, to adjust your chances to find the good outcome. We each know what it feels like to miss a chance, this comes from knowing it was there but not acted upon with the skill available to us. Or that sometimes events unfold too fast we could not change the eventual outcome often to our disappointment, but note how many times things work out just fine because you rolled into them with some fortitude we call luck. This could be probability playing out. You have no probability to suddenly disappear invisibly, but you do have a chance to alter lifestyle on the planet it benefits the biological processes that create life.

There is a chance there is no God as equally a chance there is a God: neither can be said to be proven. But we can state there exists a way of life that suits and supports the sustainment of life via biological protection. And that equally there exists other negative opposing information states that kill, destroy life, these can be found in insect to insect eating each other, or animal eating each other which supports life.

Climate change factors attack and do not support life well enough within an understanding of probable outcome, where humans are destroying the biological processes in a long term probability where if temperatures rise to 3 or 4, then 5 then 6 Celsius we risk destruction of animal human insect species as a mass extinction, or part of such over the next 200 year period.

This attack is done by coal use for home, business use, travel, and agriculture methods, ice melt, and storms that disturb species habitats, or heat waves that force species to find cooler places. They cannot catch up with the rate of exchanges playing out in reality, just like you may find reality moving too quickly that you cannot adjust well enough. Yes some species do make it, but the rate at which the overall species numbers have to move is far beyond their capabilities, and this is the problem for species, and has a knock on effects for humans where crops fail due to the wrong insect balance. The end result is destructive outcome.

This fear and heavy criticism of climate change, caused by a 100 year economic platform, has to be balanced against the biological human gains during that time. Had we not used fossil fuels or not pushed the economic way ruthlessly and selfishly many of us would not have been born into a health, education, housing society as what is existent in the developed world. We may have lived in dire poverty. Or not been born at all.

Regardless of whatever it would or could have been like; once information came in citing environmental degradation the economies of the world needed to adjust and limit production and exploitation. They should have begun adjusting in the late1970's as defined and understood by the collective understandings around environment held at the United Nations. Instead they let 80% of freshwater species decline, along with 60% of mammals. They chose money over environment. And this was pushed on as an agenda via business and university brains creating laws to suit profits including exploitation of developing countries' natural environments, leaving behind heavily degraded lands. Politicians allow exploitation to occur, such as money being channelled through tax havens which cost the poor nations 5 trillion dollars the first decade this century.

This stops local governments gaining tax revenue for it to spend on its own people. It also allows starvation to occur because you could have bought food for your own people. Somalia has exported food at famine times. A ruthless despicable fact of political-business-university educated custodians of free market forces.

Chapter 5

Soul

This is how you take a soul –

Encourage the human race to attack the biological system that creates all life on this planet. However, that alone cannot take a soul.

To take the soul you need agreement or committed continued actions to the process. So if light force or God wants your soul IT would have to strike agreement. Hold a distinction of information that if explained to you through religion or via other means establishes what you have to do in order for your soul to be taken by God. Or we might say Heaven. Or by angels. Or by higher constructive forces. Higher probability fields.

The commitment to follow the principles within a religion allow the individual a mental security and self reassurance that they will end up with God or some realm called heaven, or a next better life if Buddhist.

The other side is destructive, where dark forces and so called degraded entities, demons, or fallen angels, or jinn, or other ancient terms that all mean the same thing in consequences: the probability of bad outcome. Lower probability fields. Unless you like bad outcome! I mean what is this Hell or bad karma malarkey? Do we as a civilization really know? We might guess.

Whether such things literally exist or not is not the point of focus here. These two outcomes good bad, heaven hell, as presented by religion are actually presented as a possibility. They can occur if religion is correct by their knowledge and definition. And even if you believe in one life we can say that for anyone: good or bad can occur to you and your family as a chance or probability.

This holds to the logic held around eternal reality, God reality and religious reality. In other words; a probability reality where two extremes can occur. And where there is no certainty of outcome for any individual unless high end religious virtue is followed to the good, or low end virtue to the bad, where both are understood clearly as concepts of good and evil. And where end of life outcomes (after life outcomes) would be almost certain. Which is why psychologically (we can assume) some people live an extremely religious life: they logically assume this ends well for them. They try to play the repetition of certain behaviours and thoughts that link them to God's higher intelligent enlightened realms of existence.

These links exist but are not really explained by religious literature that they are presenting links as such. They simply get on with the job that advise us as to what is best as their religion sees it.

These suggestions are their links to God. The point of the BIBLE or QURAN is to set an impression around what God wants from us. The overall impression is a structure of links. Where prayer seems to be a very important link. As does belief in afterlife, love, care and forgiveness. And more.

Chapter 6

Links to God and Satan

Okay, the Christians make the most obvious referral to a link and that is Christ 'through Christ' our lord we are one and all the same… stuff like that.

Buddhists proclaim a long list of actions and positive thoughts and meditations that link to enlightenment; you might call it the highest available consciousness that if you get, you are in.

Muslims say stuff like when referring to Jesus or Muhammad 'peace be upon him' or prayers or adoring Allah / God (that made the universe) and other practises.

By partaking in this sort of action awareness structure you are linking with what is the probability structure connected to God. This is for certain. And if not, then what are you connected to – fresh air?

The point to spiritual practise as endorsed given and insisted by religion is to link with God or God's structure that is said to be virtuous and loving and caring and in belief of an afterlife.

With Buddhism the connection is supposedly to a hierarchal reality of consciousness or some notion of better energy formations that continue into the next life for better not worse.

One point here to realize as fact: whatever you call the part of you that goes onward into the next life or continued reality must get there via a structure. What many people do: is not think it through in this way. They just know it exists and it will happen and that is good enough for them. But these people would not be affording an insight via paradigm. By which I mean a model of thought with some specific-ness that helps the mind make a choice with understanding. Do good not evil is a very simplified frame and model we all understand.

All I am saying here is that people lose some meaning and knowledge because the very process they adhere to is not entered with a specific thought to it being towards a set of structural links. Just as code, you download on the internet, like some app directs you through an internet structure, so it is when you pray or forgive or love you engage with links towards God higher probability light. But in this reality of the soul (not the internet) you also make your own bit of code, to use an analogy. And your bit of code making – like via when you love or forgive – connects to those similar codes offered you from God. Which are generally what religion cites as being ways that God prefers.

Meanwhile a scientist might argue – and to what is such a structure made of that we can detect it and measure it? The convenient answer would be that it could well lie outside the range of energy we can detect, where something like electromagnetic fields contain the information in algorithmic forms.

The details are not relevant here, just be certain you cannot leave as if through fresh air into the afterlife. Nothing wrong with thinking you do, like me why bother beyond that as a thought, but here I am forced to make some better reasoning, unless you have heard it all before… which I bet you have not. Hence what I state here: is either correct, incorrect, logical, or illogical or very possible. That is for you to decide and then as always with such things the influence of the overall group plays out. I mean if I am not saying something a bit original than why say it.

In short I will categorically state for the spiritual record: any continuation into an afterlife must occur via the transference of you as an energy information unit and unless that unit possesses specific structural similarities you cannot be taken. You have to contain recognizable information. In life you either uphold it or delete it.

And be clear here again there is no reason for any religious minded person to learn or accept what I offer here, just understand what I offer is a better way to see what you are doing, I offer a modern day description, not any alternative religion or practise to what any of you proclaim. I am merely stating that each person's belief in an afterlife and as a practise of actions to it must have a connection via physical spiritual links (albeit not all physical as what you find in 3 dimensions) to that system.

Like a car that travels a road network. Where you are the car moving along a spiritual road. Where your design of spirituality is you, the car made of things, or qualities that are also part of the things or qualities of the road.

Types of spiritual units (you) follow types of spiritual structures, is my point. If not, you are suggesting we are all the same within, regardless of virtue and a lifetime of effort to be virtuous as indeed that is what religion teaches you to do – practise virtue and morality so much it literally changes what you are inside as a spiritual entity. An entity that can produce a sports car or broken down wreck.

You can go to a Heaven or Hell, so to speak, good karma bad karma next reality. Be clear here – what entity you become as a soul / spirit / essence, or what you yourself would call it (via using links) is also within the next environment you meet that religions call Heaven. Like for like.

Meanwhile single word definitions about God can be very misleading, like for instance – God is love, or claims that we are all equal, and all will turn out well, there is nothing to fear. These are religious people spinning a misconception albeit beautifully sounding and really positive. God is beyond such words and yes we are all equal, but do not then assume all things end equal, they categorically are not. And work has to made that they do not end bad.

Religion teaches good ends and bad ends based upon its own explanations. But no, this is not good enough for some people, they have to twist and condense truths into well-meaning sound bites that detract from the simple overall message of religion. A message that if understood is a method to link you the listener to links into the afterlife that you acquire during the life process.

The continual made up modern versions with only positive spin is incorrect; because it concludes no differentiation at all, and leads a person into a false conclusion about the nature of universal reality.

So for you; this work offers no respite, and you are best served by not entertaining it. In other words you should say – I am totally wrong and trying to frighten you. Which I am not trying, (your own misdeeds that I point out here are the frightening thing, not what I say here).

I think it fair anyone with a spiritual philosophy that makes reality as a non-suffering automatic fair and square beautiful outcome; should not listen to me here. I offer no such spin. And if you bother to understand religions such as Buddhism, Christianity, Islam, Judaism, and more, they all have a potential to bad outcomes, or detours, ha-ha, not that some people have to wait too long do they – 9 million people starve to death each year.

Real religion does not proclaim any such falsehoods, about there is nothing to worry about. Real religion warns and informs of great goods and great outcomes connected to virtue. And warns of the opposite: hell states of experience. That is what they go on about and that is the overall tenet to the simple message.

Jesus saves you does he? Fine, but you best use the links he sends and you use them via virtue, love and care. Not a consumerism lifestyle that is baking the planet and is going to cause storms, floods, fires, death, destruction, starvation, and water shortages. Caused by us and handed down to tomorrow's children. That is heavenly virtue is it? Well is it? Say something in your heart – am I right or wrong? Tell me why I am wrong and then show me what religion you are and the bit of evidence from your book that shows me to be wrong. I thought you had to protect life.

Many of the religious classes do not see that climate change is a spiritual problem, they talk rubbish that God will sort it out, or there isn't a dire problem and if there is, it isn't going to affect their soul ignoring it; in turn they play no part in climate change reforms. No, for religion: virtue links, belief links have warped into a conceit that only their religion is correct and only their main man (never a woman) can save them. Oh sorry, I forgot Mary.

If you look around here some people suffer others do not. We cannot say this outcome is anything to do with virtues. But it shows the probabilistic nature of reality on Earth. And that all outcomes here are very varied. You can also say that if you do practise virtue and it strengthens you it doesn't matter what you get hit with as regards terrible outcomes your spiritual components shine and create insight, intelligence, conscience, strength, conscientiousness, empathy, love – stuff they call the riches of heaven. With these types of qualities it can be said people are powerful because these types of qualities construct the entity we might call soul or spirit or some essence, you might have another term you understand that I am not using here. The point is by virtue, love, reflection, kindness and so forth qualities you create a spiritual unit that is the equivalent to a sports car. A car that will meet and greet and travel into an afterlife reality. Somewhere in that car is instruction from God and agreement to God: links of information states energies that guide you if you use the right decoder via virtue, love, patience and so forth.

We aren't controlled by God as an information state – doesn't sound anywhere as great as God is love, I grant you that. What we receive is not a control mechanism we are not robots we have free will. It is like being given code and re using it as you see fit and suited within your culture. I mean if you live 100 thousand years ago virtue would play out differently and would be more basic around survival. You may not be too polite to strangers or loving to wild animals as they could be a threat to your life.

If all is information then the connection to God through God is through information states. Such links are not only the written word they are another (*word*) instruction written in the heart as soul. If Buddhist then you say; energy information states that you actually cannot avoid and where the configurations are favourable to unfavourable constructions. High low probability mixes. That is where your religion tells you to focus, whereas Christianity and Islam are arguably focused upon the creator of those constructs. That is how it seems if we compare Christianity and Islam to Buddhism.

I cannot exclude Buddhist thought here because they lack a God. Because they adhere to following high virtue states to obtain good karma conditions from reality. They just do not focus on a notion that God made that reality. As if anyone knows what God is or is not by definition. You know do you? Well if you know tell everyone and let's see how many definitions you have? I assume those descriptions will be the same? Creator of universe and Heaven and Angels is my definition here. Where IT – God, sends information states to all forms and where the tangle of information states is the universe and where the universe creates its own information states that I regard as probability states, the control of which all humans play a part in by their everyday actions, thought feelings, and intentions.

Use those links this universe sends you from God, is my appeal to you here, or ignore them at your peril, or lot of aggravation. When we ignore them we go into a different type of time calculation system where we find ourselves fret and pressured by time with not enough of it to find the answer.

There are probability structures floating about the algorithmic airwaves or different code that quite literally run ruin upon unsuspecting souls like a random event where you have significant disadvantages, but where it is suddenly your duty or call of fate to process those information probability structures.

They don't exist? No – how about every accident that occurs that occurs across the world daily? You didn't design them or ask for them or will them to you, they are random built in a societal probability reality of our making. Make cars you make crashes. Make cigarettes you make cancer. Make alcohol you make drunks some of which randomly kill by driving. All held in predictable probabilities. Alter the alcohol consumption rate you alter the drunk rate and alter the deaths by car rate.

Listen to God information about not being greedy and selfish and ruthless or glutinous you end up in a different collective probability state where there is less obesity, less inequality, less violence, less starvations to death. And no environmental destruction and pollution as we now have to live within.

Destruction caused via the business political law makers, who use an average human mind set structured by greed habits found in culture, but where they cheated themselves and as many people as possible to make as much money as possible. The only difference between their collective greed and ours is that they exploited for bigger money, bigger power, but which they cannot be called evil with intent at a conscious level, only that seek you shall find, like for like – greedy today becomes greedy tomorrow with more incentive to pass diabolical laws around tax and pollution allowance and environmental destruction. Like a weightlifter on steroids a monster in the making. Gulping up as much they can. The outcome – billionaire culture. Created by the UN and EU world government structures based around probabilities that focus on money and arms control. Only then will the UN protect the earth, its people, animals, and insects.

Lose the insects you lose crops and people starve. Protection is in the details; understood in environmental studies and put conveniently under the table of doom, upon which sits international war councils and helter-skelter international companies.

If you leave business people to do as they want they won't pay tax and they will, via educated people from universities, argue in courts and create laws to suit these lawless business elites bent on creation of wealth for themselves. This was all held in probabilities. What you thought they would listen to religion and its texts on not to be greedy? Or that they would listen to the soul God gave them? Ha, don't be silly they ignore some information for other information that is a different probability structure and by doing so gives them advantages to make more money. If they were fair they would not be so rich. If you want to be very rich you can't be too fair and honest around tax. You cheat it to what the laws allow that other greedy people made for you.

These people did not invent greed they picked it up in general culture. Understood in a Bible and Quran context we call it Satanic, but this is a dated term, it is merely a word for a lower probability states or lower energies information states with lower calculation tools and inventions opposing the higher state we might say leads to God and the virtues of that kind which are not based on greed. Low spiritual IQ you might call it, but where the agency goes beyond the minds' of humans.

These lower states can be said to exist upon Earth at some atomic level that is lower vibration albeit not detectable by science, but which if calculated is decidedly different to higher probability states. Virtue is naturally challenged by these states where the individual goodness and signal within, is like a sweetness caught by bitterness.

Toughen up stiffen up and jump ahead with as much positive motion you can, you never know you might scream – praise the lord! Found by the religious at heart who appreciate life experience normally with a degree of reflection for creation by some thing we are told to call God.

Look how rude and angry and hateful many of us can be at times as shown on social media which leads to suicides by right of those types of probability structures. Invent more quantities of rudeness you increase the chances of death via suicide and rage that leads to violence. Create more love, as the great late Jesus taught, you create more chance of laughter sharing equality hope and energy for one and other. Instead we went on a walk down the dark side of reality – guns, bombs, porn, drugs, obesity addiction and so on states of behaviour.

Now look – climate change is merely a dimension of greediness. Too higher a consumption rate, born from a political economic mechanism around feeding the body and passions with stuff made from atoms and importing into minds the desire for those things. Where soon there is an attaching of enjoyable feelings to those wants for atom objects. The wanting: is where the feeling is – not in the objects themselves. The use and holding of the objects makes us feel good. The objects might hold some status or practical use and understood by the mind produces appreciative feelings. This process is the state at play for all of us.

We hold on to that process chained to the habits of doing things and we will suffer the moral and spiritual consequences for what further could be said to also be a type of system repetition: habit for a way of life, a style of doing things that involve how we heat our homes, energise our businesses, muster our farming practises and travel by cars and so forth. To be a modern day human we have to understand this political business structure is leading us into climate change doom and gloom. We have to then understand that to solve this problem we need politicians and business to restructure transport and building and farming to green energy saving methods.

Individuals cannot meet climate targets, only political business forces can. Without this transference of structural methods there is no climate solution. And currently the changing over to the solutions is too slow hence we find ourselves within a climate emergency.

Society in order to have active links to God in relation to climate change would need to understand that politicians acting too slow must be morally objected to.

Most people in all societies do not understand this imperative social reaction, we just assume we can live our lives in trust of politicians which has a practical sense to it – I mean why should people have to learn about climate science, climate policy, climate society?

Alas we do have to learn something of these things held in a one concept meaning: and that is – we must stick to climate targets and to do so must pressurise all governments to do so, without this action we cannot be said to have a link to God via climate change.

Many people will assume the links to God would be the individual actions like going vegan or walking to work and countless other actions. Yes they are right to some degree, but these individual actions cannot meet the climate targets, so all you are doing is sustaining the lower probability dark force reality religion calls Satan in its books. A complex system that acts to destroy life.

Remember; climate change literally is the attack upon the creation life giving structure. And misguided political thinking and old fashioned out of date thinking; is the crucifying element to stop positive change to create sophisticated society.

If we had stuck with all the ideas of old we would not have cars or phones or televisions. If we stick with the ideas of old around transport, farming and energising business and so forth, we stick with climate change which is an economic killing machine, which said in relation to God is Satan – or said in modern terms – dark force, lower, slower moving probability structure, that acts to kill life.

If society thinks and acts in these dark force terms society will be led into killing. And if Satan is to really have its way it would attack creation itself. Climate change supported by slow moving policies supported by a general public that allows politicians to move too slow suits Satan not God.

So the Satanic force at its most powerful end loads its system into an in-depth slow moving slow changing awareness system, called consciousness, in humans. Satan relies upon religion holding an out of depth old fashioned definition as to what Satan is and means, when used in the Bible and Quran. Once so, religious society does not define or think of itself as enforcing Satan ways in what can be called complex links. Where the link to Satan here is the allowing politicians to move too slow to climate change policies.

A typical reader of the Quran and Bible has been forwarded a set of words and meanings that create a meme cultural state of society minds, linking it to the understanding and definitions of centuries old.

A meme is a term for cultural understood meanings; where a communication between minds occurs in an easy to transfer way. This may involve slang, images, music tunes, symbols. A meme state today understands what robots are, DNA, and recently popular term blah, blah, blah, dance moves, fight moves in movies and video games where kids copy-cat the moves playing around. None of this existed 100 years ago, or themes like save the planet. Or academic notation and even certain body languages like slapping hands or waves goodbye.

Memes are a complex of meanings styled together, that probably transfer at quick speed, allowing the receiver and the giver of the message / meaning: quick understanding. Thank you so much, maybe a thumbs-up or smiling face emoji.

To use another definition from **Meme – Wikipedia** – 'A meme is an idea, behaviour, or style that spreads by means of imitation from person to person within a culture and often carries symbolic meaning representing a particular phenomenon or theme. A meme acts as a unit for carrying cultural ideas, symbols, or practices, that can be transmitted from one mind to another through writing, speech, gestures, rituals, or other imitable phenomena with a mimicked theme. Supporters of the concept regard memes as cultural analogues to genes in that they self-replicate, mutate, and respond to selective pressures'.

In simplest words all I am saying here, in Biblical Quran meme speak, is that we are selling our souls to Satan via climate change. Said in intellectual reasoning terms, I am saying that our souls as defined as some internal power as a spiritual power is something to do with the power to reinforce life with beauty and love and care and joy; hence in these things the link to God.

Climate change causes ugliness to natural settings like a dying forest, dried up lakes, desperation in starving humans and species, hate, wars over natural resources, biological disturbances like Covid-19 where the species diversity, when cut down, allows natural disease jumps to occur from animal to humans.

The list grows where the natural reflective abilities of a human that can be said to be highly sensitive and moral and spiritually loving are challenged and trashed by dark force structures that do not encourage the use of those qualities, but encourage via distraction or attraction the use of anger, rage, hate, violence, rudeness, selfishness, drug porn addiction, materialistic wants like fancy cars, jewellery, the prestige of certain clothes and so on. All these things and many more take our time energy thoughts reflections and given a wrong balance, compared to the soul qualities I described, do cause us problems as a social group. The phenomena of these problems via disproportion mechanics is Satan.

The things like drugs, porn, violence, hate, jewels, and fancy lifestyles are not in themselves evil dark or Satan phenomena. They are legitimate human expressions to which to entertain the self through time, to pass the time. But it has to be said if society put the same energy and efforts into helping humans we would not allow 9 million to starve each year. And the world would be a different place. As it is we do need to hate sometimes or get angry and be selfish, crude and ruthless, and dress slick and expensive. All these things have a valid place in society and fit the inventions of the self through the ages. These things are as natural to us as love is or kindness. But when you as an individual decide to tip most of your personal balance away from the light qualities you will maintain darkness and you will reflect it to yourself in thoughts, emotions to others, and tolerance of a political system aiding climate change and its consequences.

Your intentions will always be good but accompanying your intensions are your actions. And here we see the fat from overeating or the drinker or smoker all messed up overdoing these things. Your intentions were not to be fat, an alcoholic, or supporter of climate that goes against God's creation, so you mean well. But what you want and mean and hope for, compared to what you get and what you cause, are two very different things sometimes. Where your will comes into play, where your ability to force issues comes into play; to take control and find direction.

As a society in relation to climate change we risk destroying society as we know it at moral temperatures that have been set at 1.5 and 2 Celsius, we might add to that scope and say 2.4 Celsius one day. As it stands no one has asked the world's people to decide the temperatures of morality. The science and political community decided it for us in the 2015 Paris climate agreement. As an individual or country you may well decide on an adjusted moral temperature based upon your own clear understanding, but remember at 6 Celsius which has a 10% chance to occur, at which point you can forget civilisation as you know it, and it is that responsibility we living in the 2020's have to strategize to, right now. Push too slow too late darkness will mar our souls and whole Islands like the Bahamas will go under water at around 2 Celsius and beyond.

Meanwhile the objects of God are not atoms they are virtues and beliefs about an afterlife. These are two very opposite types of links. Yes we need both, but there is not much power in hoarding a long list of atomic objects when compared to hoarding qualities of the heart and soul; that can transfer across more dimensions of time and space than what we know of here on Earth. If you don't understand that then you don't understand what religion is all about – fighting against the attraction speed and orbit of an atomic system.

Where the more atomic system you have pervading the self the more likely you are to exist in realities of that system into an afterlife. All notions of such being called Hell is an old fashioned image out of date description and sound-bite. You cannot be in hell if suited to wherever you end up in. A fish is made for the sea a bird for the sky. A baby has very suitable awareness to mix wonderfully with other babies much better than adults who for all their intelligence have very limited baby social skills. Ten babies together get along fine in their high chairs screaming and crying and making noise with their own shared group understanding.

In the afterlife, if different structures exist; then I am certain the nearest structures to what Earth is made of, call it lower heavens, is nearest as a literal location. (Note very carefully *location* is not a spatial location as we understand and experience it, but rather sets of locations everywhere) (Where the location is an information state and you are part of that information state.) Where you as a soul / spirit / essence (or whatever you wish to call it) will go those places suited to your souls type of awareness. Where you then have senses and abilities suited to those environments. Where further up to highest heavens are structures made of orbits that are not eventually atomic in any form. What religion calls: of the spirit. And like I said earlier – objects of God are all about virtues and qualities like love: there are no atoms there. So there won't be any atoms in highest heavens.

When any religion insists of afterlife pain and suffering – it is the pain of reflection. Reflecting in the knowledge sensitive to what a soul has become. And where it is clear that what one has become is a shadow of what one should have become. Or worse: all of what one had, as given to them by God, was thrown away.

Make no ifs and buts – being forced to look back seeing what was lost and where you caused pain to others, albeit innocently more often than not, is no easy thing. And if for any reason you don't believe what I just told you, then I have to ask what is it you think you do when you land in the next reality? The pain is in the refection. And the only cheat around that is if you become that empty and dead inside there is no refection in terms of using love empathy and joy.

An atheist might then jibe – but surely the all loving God would cast another loving soul into that empty being? No, is the answer. And anyone who teaches and believes that no such empty poor souls do not exist, as if spiritual reality is all joy love and wonder, then look around, for I say with all certainty – Earth has the mixed qualities of all heavens and all hells floating through here as part of our reality. I suggest to you, whoever you are, you pick up the objects of love, care, joy and happiness, hope and energy for an eternal future, rather than wallow around in objects and a distant thought that there might be an afterlife with no faith or feeling for that future.

I am not at all religious, but at least the true religious person makes a hearty attempt at pursuing this faith and qualities of the heart and soul. Remarkable considering there is not one shred of proof bar the claims of people like Jesus, Muhammad, Buddha, about this afterlife. But pursue it they do, as indeed many a non-believer will pursue those loving qualities found in the soul. The non-believer just never sees the end result framed in the mind: eternity. The believer also has scant understanding about details only that IT (the afterlife exists) and you go there.

Any religious person thinking that a God given soul is limited because that person does not believe in an afterlife is missing the point; that a soul can be bettered by the practise with skill of love, joy, appreciation for all found in creation, like a mother and baby with its powerful engaging love and bond. But no, some people want to insist that a mere sheer belief in a religion, or one man of a religion – is of greater power than he or she; who without that belief, is using their soul as God intended at every moment. This is incorrect corrupted thinking – as if the soul God gave would be solely reliant upon a belief in one religion any religion or any man. No – and I will show why it is incorrect thinking and teaching.

Suppose I believe in the one true religion or the one true man, and yet at every moment I am bad. Meanwhile a loving caring person for all their life good at every turn – does not believe in God or religion. You are to tell us that God favours the bad person who believes in God, above the good person who does not believe in God?

Then tell me why it is I have seen God-believing people who I know have no real soul and have many a bad. Why, did reality destroy their soul? Why are they bad if believing in God or if religion is so good? Would not belief in God or religion then also make them good and keep the soul?

No, the soul contains the agreement and contract and messaging from God and it is tested at every moment through life in all sorts of ways that strengthen it and better it, that the person can then do great deeds with that power. Like opposing the evil deeds of an evil person who by chance happens to believe in religion and God, but helps to destroy this earth and its people via war and greed of money, climate destruction and any other type of bad we could name here. You would choose the evildoer who believes in God above the good doer who does not believe in God? Then go live in Syria with their leader. He believes in God.

If you believe that it is necessary for a person to have a belief in God or afterlife, or religion; and that is the only key to bettering the soul then you know nothing about the soul and its power and what it relies upon. You would limit all spiritual reality as mere belief and render all human ideals and meaning as nothing more than to be a believer in what is religion, afterlife, and God.

You would have it that when a person dies they would not then be in a great place even though they possess a great soul? No, you with religious belief about heaven and God, I too believe, but I promise you no higher place there just on mere belief, for I say she or he who acted better, as good than you, will have the higher place, bar some technical difference understood by angels and God.

Do not assume the technical difference is a belief in a God or religion or a man of that religion, that it would definitely save you from lower standing. Practise the use of your soul and then we might see some standing above those who do not practise.

You can believe what you want, it won't bring food and water to your table – you have to go and earn it or rely on charity. You earn what is in your soul and your encounter with life uploads your soul during this process of encounters and efforts in which you become what you are for that lifetime.

But given you might have many lives the overall code of what you are would surely be the whole line of your history. And that history would somehow transmit itself into reality now in this one life. We all possess different variations of belief held as possibilities. None of us know for certain what exact definitions are 100% correct in their religious claims.

That said, suppose you have no inclination to any such claims I make, then no trouble, have we here, with me. For, in your religion is surely great measure advice and insight about how to use the soul and follow true to your great leader of your religion who has shown what it takes to fulfil the soul.

That said, be clear you non-believers, I will tell you here regardless of what awaits as truth and reality, the reason for a continuing discord with a belief in an afterlife is one made around the logic found in reason and experience. By which I mean; we have acquired such reason in our cultural experience the very structures we have built reality and society have been raised by what can be proven and tested to exist as a use.

There are more users of that reasoning process you might call empirical, and uses for it than faith or hope in a scientifically unproven reality called God, afterlife, heaven, and soul, and angels. Hence logically, as more aeons pass, more evidence would have been acquired to substantiate that there is no sign of God, or proof of such has there been. Which the logical mind finds suspicious and will follow where this type of evidence leads. Right the way to not believing in God or an afterlife.

The very mechanisms of the brain will, and have sided already: with notions it is much more virtuous and honest to see religion as a cultural form with nice intentions, but no truths to be taken as a revelation given by those sent by God. Once so; soon or eventually, the academic scientific man will, without doubt, point away from any reason to believe in God, as does at every moment, an object or invention unconsciously show you the power of human creation, and the power of what can be shown to exist as an objective truth, nullifying eventually a belief in unseen unproven realities, as if superstition and out of date old fashioned thought processes and ideas are all there is to religion.

So my religious friends, or those that like me simply believe in God and or an afterlife – the modern day thought process backed up by the high scoring logical minds cultivated within the university process will eventually have it that only what has been proven to exist does exist. That is their virtue and habit. Understood be it take a thousand years or more they would have this thought to do away with any notion of a prayer to an invisible unseen God, and belief and culture of an afterlife. Just so you know you religious people where your enemy lives: in the modern scientific thought process.

They who did overthrow superstition now lead like modern day intellectual Witches, where their spells of good sound reasoning we must follow. Or else be cast aside like Jesus, Muhammad, and Buddha who do not matter to them when it comes to any notion of an afterlife. These intellectual reasoners will though follow religion, because it is culturally civilised to do so. You will hear them proclaiming truths around love, equality, fairness, and all the rest of it that is like that, but they no more believe in God or afterlife than Einstein or Hawking the science geniuses. They only believe in what can be and has been proven. It is as simple as that.

And with it just like you reading this, my little sister, so it is you may well believe climate change is no spiritual thing for you to be concerned. Be warned and warned again about me: I am no preacher – believe what you want and go where it takes you, I have never been found like Jesus on the mount, Buddha under his tree, or Muhammad with long tuition with the Arc angel Gabriel. No – more chance of finding me in a betting shop. And here I say I will be proven more right in these words here, and bet on it, than any your words that state climate change is no spiritual thing, or that we must follow one man, or one religious idea or else. Or else what? Go on bore us.

Explain why one man or one religion will save us, and what you mean so that everyone can hear it. And abruptly ignore it, but as I say – what you believe in these matters, matters-not to me, better you learn where it takes you and see it in reality just as a scientist would approve than live it and see it not.

For where is the proof in your claims of one man or one religion; where? That it take the place of he or she who practises the good loving way unifying with peace and empathy for others. You say, do you; that your religion can outweigh that amount of virtue? Or is it really the case that in your religion are countless virtues that if followed save the soul?

If the latter then this is all God means in words found in your book. You say not? Well, sister, let us then see what happens to he or she who is bad, but believes by default that by being religious is saved from darkness. For I say to you in God's garden such a person is a weed. Let us also see what happens to those who do not believe in God or religion, but practise good virtue at every day. Such a person is a flower.

Follow your soul and the links God sends is my shortest of answers. Follow them not and you will find out what the Devil is – to coin a term of phrase. You might choose a more cultured term or modern term like low probability field. And find there later it has all you could imagine attached to it, given likelihood. This term low probability field I would encourage. As I encourage and respect any religion that warns of bad ending states that cause boring realities with not many options.

But of course the modern arc of spirituality will have it: All is love. All will end well. If so, I challenge all calls to that into the afterlife where you will see differently to that totally false handicapped belief, you may as well say you can do all evil and by believing in Jesus all automatic rights into the heavenly realms are assured.

Meanwhile, also, the modern take is love, light energy, replacing the word and meaning from Jesus. I would prefer a Christian to you any day, at least they claim there is a hell, but no you modern teachers would have it only everlasting joy exists. Are you then too afraid to tell God that in the universe has hells and suffering? Then let me do it for you –

Dear God, there is suffering and hell in your universe. I offer Syria and Yemen as examples and 9 million humans who starve to death each year. And I put it to you, you only made the universe set in a realm of probabilities. As for here so elsewhere places exist beyond this life. Answer me, God, that I know the answer and how to say it. Such is my prayer to you.

So you see praying to God for me is not as you would have it by religion. As if God is far and beyond talking to. Words are words and need no church or mosque to say them to God. As if only through religion. Or as if good deeds were only then to he or she that prays. So it is this world has run towards where all those prayers meant well, (to that I pay full respect) but where other things brought so bad, like war and destruction of the flesh and the soul; of those doing and living the hating. For so it is we live in probabilities. And one of like produces another of like and soon they join and emerge to greet us, just as once germs were not known to exist, so it is I say to you reading this; probabilities exist to help you or destroy you.

Hence it was surely always likely, hell would appear. Or the Devil himself! For the universe is only a probability or set of them. And who is it that controls such? With proof it is humans who control Earth, and so like climate change, bad is the fault of humans not some fictitious conscious bad entity corrupting the souls from you, other than it be the emergence properties within probabilities.

It is the will of humans that direct the probabilities in the main, and cause reality as we know it in society. And so far all we have had from the religious flock is quiet voices around climate change. No urgency, no claim of relinquishing the soul if we relinquish the species, no cry of loyalty to God's creation. And so it may well be we will lose this Earth to what? Greed is the word here on this Earth not the word of God. Two very different codes. Yes, no? Speak. But please do not bore us with the same old messages and quotes whilst you all watch the planet burn. Because if you do that (which you currently are you religious people) you will surely save your soul via prayer but leave behind a ruined biological system with lost species and lost humans.

That is your fate and I who write these words am the first to tell you – such is my virtue.

<h1 align="center">Chapter 7</h1>

<h1 align="center">Algorithms</h1>

Can an algorithm be evil? Or loving? Or protective of the human race? Can it take your soul? Replenish your soul? It can give you information. What information you seek it shall provide. What adverts it offers are a side issue. The information you seek is key to the algorithm outcome.

SEO is search engine optimization. It basically means if people are going to find your website there has to be certain electronic coded links that allow this. So if you sell sports shoes and someone puts in their search box 'white trainers' you want Google to take them to your website. Ha-ha-ha good luck with that. That's like relying upon the Devil to take you to Heaven; you can expect a long hard detoured ride that suits the Devil.

Millions of other sites will also be trying to get the same person to their website, and only the first 10 or 20 businesses that come up on the answers, Google give, get looked at more or less. And you could be hundreds of pages down on the list.

I mean, suppose you live in a small place like Lingfield and have a sports shop and someone puts in their search box – trainers from

Lingfield, you will come up on the first list Google offer because there will not be that many sports shops in the area. But generally internet business is to receive payment from anywhere and then post the item on to anywhere. And when not this configuration; is still having to abide to getting noticed more than the competition.

And so people will not even name a town they just type in something like – 'white trainers size 42' or variation of instruction for Google to use to then show them white trainers. Your business will never be on the first pages. And although it is free to unravel the system you are likely to fail is my point, it can take years of effort which if you were to succeed would probably make you rich. The only other way is to pay for your site to be noticed and this then is no different to other advertising where the bigger companies will out-perform your small budget.

In short, it is about how you present your website in codes and other very complex managing issues. Like connection and use to social media or how often you update information. The list is like trying to solve an almost impossible Sudoku or crossword puzzle.

Ask anyone in business SEO is really hard for them. Am I saying it is wrong, no it is a remarkable cultural business phenomenon. But a part of me literally wonders if a part of it is literally evil. This is abject control of peoples hopes, fears, ambitions, desperation, albeit it cultivates observation and intelligence and creativity, I am not opposed to this, but if you ask people with websites what they think about the hell of SEO they will say how challenging it is and how you have to go down an electronic designed world that can seem soul destroying in time, hopes, fears, and ultimately money. Because in the end they hook you into getting around the system by paying for their sophisticated codes to help you via what they call key words.

SEO is a mind control way of life culture; encouraging people in the business world to go along the yellow brick algorithm road and electronically sell part of their soul for a place on the first page heaven of Google.

This goes way beyond a simple pay to get your 'shop' noticed, which is arguably painless, whilst this is signing up to a cult of electronic wonderland.

How many first pages are there? Can you climb Mount Everest?

My advice – go to those who claim they have what we might call a degree in SEO and save your soul from one of the most abusive misleading psychological hooks of all time.

These geeks behind its structure are not after your money, but your thought process behind your actions. They even have a dark side called black hat tactics that if you employ they will literally punish you like the Devil itself might. You will be barred or placed a long way away from the first set of results. And often businesses do not always understand that these tactics have been employed by the agencies they ask to construct their business system. When Google spot the cheating tactic punishment is dished out. It is as simple as that. Algorithms show no mercy they do as instructed and do not listen to your innocent complaints that you only employed a guy to help you advertise.

What these super companies are bringing to the world is mind soul control and I am really sorry for a million lost souls chasing the dragon in the god of SEO.

And after the chase, the Googles' of this world have left countless companies deeply buried in their own innocent mistakes: no attention from their magical algorithms. And suddenly no goods are purchased online because Google ignore your code structure. All because you couldn't unravel the maize.

As you read a website algorithms will be observing you, and listing what you look at and for how long and how this applies to others doing the same. Those with the habits held in the largest group are of particular interest because here lies the key to learning what makes these people tick: how they engage with internet content.

So what algorithms then have to work out from the observation is how to sell you something or present some more of what you are looking at with another advert flashed your way. This is going on all day, millions of algorithmic acts going on behind the scenes for ever more.

When you search online Google will have a set of algorithms latched onto it taking you to a destination, whilst taking your information about you to its own analysis system, and further selling your information around preferences to other buyers of information and other owners of algorithms. It is a dark hidden world. I am not saying get rid of algorithms. Just know they are there to aid us and manipulate us. In the end they use aiding us, to manipulate us and to make someone richer. They are responsible for making us addicted to information content as a way of life. This is their soul deceiving trick. Hence you see everyone looking at a phone screen more than ever before in public places whilst in the company of other people. We are literally in competition with phones to keep the attention of who we are sharing our company with. And the phone often wins.

We spend hours observing information, entertainment communication, buying or selling – algorithms own that observed material on you. They know what humans do. And then they play a part in having a relationship with us. Yes humans design the algorithms and direct their general use to search data and come up with all sorts of answers beyond just what we encounter and use on the internet. Like in missile systems, analysis for medical reasons, science and all sorts of good. But it cannot be denied we now live within an algorithmic web. We are caught in it for life on Earth. Even if you never use the internet, algorithms are playing a part in all around you. And a lot of this part is governed by the New World Destructive Order. And they will observe you or they will advertise to you and they will make you create more greenhouse gas emissions via travel, stuff you buy, and your addictions to meat which is18%, of worldwide CO2 emissions.

It is worth noting here, that even people totally unconnected to the internet cannot escape the internet web, it is there in the world directing things just as a religious person understands God is there directing and influencing things unseen unknown to the non-believer.

The internet is paid for by money. From owning and controlling valuable information that a person does not understand the value of and gives away for free. That is the price. I am not making complaint to this inherent principle. We either pay with money or some other commodity, and it is the other commodity (our information) we pay with. Oddly enough a very efficient commodity almost genius in its format because it is much quicker to transfer than money and needs no evaluation from the user as with the use of money – hence it has a quick to multiply growth factor attached to it. This is the natural outcome of its system as it uses more bits of analysis creating more observed values than what humans can even understand.

The algorithm systems have to be allowed to work out their own ways of doing analysis often based upon simple rules given by the human coders. So what the algorithm system is: is a value system of information. And I am not being critical of this. It is intelligence at work. I am merely stating IT will and must and is… making us buy more goods like robots or slaves to its measure. And if the Devil were to ever incarnate that is where IT lives. Because there – the internet – if it can keep driving us forward to buy more and more: which is what it does, IT will cause more CO_2 emissions via the increased production of goods. The algorithmic state literally invents new ways to hook us into a sensory information state that has secret agencies or carriers of your time and attention to buy something. Nothing is free. All is paid for. By us.

In the end super companies like Amazon or Google will have a system so complete efficient and powerful IT will have deeply hidden analysis systems coming at the individual that are so forceful so connected to us that push pulls into our senses will make it likely we do certain things above other things. Understood it is no different to how casinos understand probabilities and where all bets available act to defeat the complex of all players in the end. But here in Google World it is like playing a chess supercomputer where it knows how to keep playing you for as long as possible sending you down the rabbit hole to a buy product end. Along the way extracting as much information from you as is possible valuable to its system of analysis. I mean, we cannot say to an algorithm structure stop at some given point. That would go against the very principle that it is.

Played out elsewhere away from the internet such analysis allows breakthroughs in science and technology. CERN particle collider or GENOME project are simple examples.

But on the internet it is like a sophisticated psychological analysis of you. Where we get placed into different groups showing the internet systems who buys what and what triggers those buy end results. In the end this becomes some function of production in goods and services in relation to our time and work and toil to produce goods and services. The funnel off is cheaper goods for more people and a few more billionaires and well paid geek coders. Their billions is not the issue here. I mean if you want to become a buying machine via the agency of the internet I don't really care as a personal care. But here as an observation to spiritual insight for anyone who reads this we go back to religion and the words like greed and gluttony. That is what this type of system is building into: our thought feeling processes. And what you have to understand is that as a collective we are coded by God.

The world in life forms all follow a purpose via codes to their existence that makes each species exist; and all that balances out to afford us to continue as a life system. In which if you attend those codes around morality, care, love, forgiveness, and thanks to God – the thing that gave us existence – we create a very different reality by solving problems within the system of life. Because if we spent all day thinking of ways to help others and then commit to actions, the world would be almost perfect. If we, on the other extreme, spent all day thinking how to get rich or buy more and more goods we would never help people in need and the world would be hell in ruthlessness.

As a system of souls during that life process we try to acquire the needed information that aids us to further knowledge and sophistication as a value into the next life or afterlife. Hence spiritual systems like religion have an inherent value that they focus time and attention upon doing good for spiritual reality however your religion defines it. By that sort of work and toil seen in your morality you attune the soul, re-create the soul the information state to God. In short it is obvious to me, anyone with this ideology – so long as afterlife exists – must have some advantage above the lesser searching of the non-religious person. What challenges believers is their own limitations to exist in a complex world where religious values cannot comprehend the natural emergence of what in energy terms (similar to what Einstein understood to limited degree) is all about the natural power of atom reality and its orbits. I mean; God made the universe with atoms is my point, but the soul is not made of atoms.

What carries a human evolvement through long stretches of time is the ability to transcend the previous information state held in your parents' time, or the parent structure before that. If not we would still be wandering the earth by horse and cart or walking picking berries, without books, cars, planes, and even clothes! We do not want to live in the past. But let me tell you something – if our ancestors who lived 20 thousand years ago saw a video of our war exploits, they would sit in cold disturbed silence. A state of spiritual shock. I mean how could you contemplate what we as a group can destroy? compared to those innocent days. And worse – now we have an un-beautifully arranged chance by the business government forces structured way of life, to wipe out the biological order. That is where we all sit. And what every person has to understand, is that they each contribute a scale of loading information into the system.

I cannot under any circumstances, whatsoever, say a vagrant has less input than a President as a value to God. All contribute to an information soul system where each is juggling virtue held in the reactions of their heart. And where a President may well fail miserably compared to the vagrant because that powerful man on earth never understood the values of heaven: to love, care, give, take, and accept fate with a loving heart: God's system and we navigate it via codes told to us in the holy books. We do not buy into it via a cash payment or being greedy. We buy out of it by being greedy, we lessen our power.

What takes a soul to the dark side low probability state or light side high probability state has nothing to do with how we view power here. Real spiritual power is a juggling act how you manage your time with what you have got and to do so with a light free loving heart. A man with a million dollars who gives to charity is not necessarily giving more from the heart than one who gives a dollar to the beggar in the street, with a kinder feeling and heart. And cannot steal a place into the power of spiritual realms and awareness as well the beggar.

God system and reality as known by Jesus very well understood these secret functions – he just reflected it naturally. This makes him very powerful and one to be reckoned with. Such a heart cannot be beat. Because that is what it is all about; codes to God.

Chapter 8

How to kill a lot of HUMANS

Military spending is 800 000 million USA dollars, climate change spending 10 000 million.

It is a perfect reflection of our world balance. War and destruction over construction. 80 times more spent on war than climate change. A balance and recipe for destruction. With no realistic likelihood of world war we still cannot unhinge from this habit.

But as with all factors that go on around the world it has a mind-set of logic connected to it: the idea to defend one's own country. And two world wars prove this necessity. But again the spending amount is so great the business – a thriving industry – it attracts the ultimate greed power psyche from big business. They have the power of a thousand Greta Thunbergs to influence the world. She and all climate campaigners and all politicians cannot stop the rise in emissions spinning towards 2.5 degrees. All between is hot air. With 800 000 million up for grabs, do not expect the arms business and their mind-set to be encouraged to stop. Yes, these war mobs, with their armies, can kill humans, but not as efficiently as the collective tipping point output of CO_2 emissions.

However, atom bombs are capable of wiping out most of all humans, if you drop thousands of them. Leaders will not give up these weapons because of the mind-set and logic of how the New World Destructive Order works. It is a mind-set where each individual connected to it is also constructive hence a contradictory illusion exists, where civility, education, democracy, and other structures subject us to see the well-meaning and constructive conscious intent of such people.

However, the overall direction is down and is an emergence from the overall collective of systems that have no real controller other than see what happens and hope for the best. Humans do not sit hoping to murder the human race. Alas for us we don't have to we have climate change to give us a gamblers chance.

Leaders hope for a positive end and process, and so too do many aspects of business serve us with medicine, technology, education, banks, and business structures that create jobs, buy homes, and clothe our children. To what degree business structures could have fed the world better and not caused climate change is conjecture now, and no point in looking back to where the key mistakes were.

Countries waged 2 world wars and the UN acted to stop such ends, and in so doing expanded industry and knitted us together via economic structures and ideas. Then took their eye off the environment and now we sit with a 5% chance, or so, to wipe out billions of humans via starvation and heat as we impact upon the ecological food chain, which is another way of saying; the structure of all species eating bits of each other involving plants, insects, animals, all there ultimately to serve human survival and consumption.

It's a flow, a mechanism with tight parameters that if you step outside, which is not easy to do, wipes out life as we know it. Understood in its fuller picture billions have a right and likelihood to be born and then in so doing go to an afterlife. Half the world believes in this afterlife half do not. So the half can consider this and will in the future whilst the other half will dismiss it as pure fantasy, but still logical if looked at coldly – there isn't proof an afterlife exists, nor does not. It is possible and that is all we know and can prove. That is the key point here – we can prove an afterlife is possible because there are no ways to prove otherwise.

Had Jesus and Muhammad come now they would have had a hard time convincing the modern mind of an afterlife and judging God: people would have asked for proof or that an angel appear or some other modern variant of logic. As it is culture has loaded within it ideas and calculations that God does exist. So you and I believe it, just as others disbelieve it, but none can prove it as not existing – both sides rely upon belief.

And what cannot be denied or ever beaten is the way information structures create human thought and helps to construct human society education and culture and communication. We change generation to generation, but we literally hand down information beliefs, facts, and hopes and plans. These cultural information states are in buildings, films, books, personality traits, and all generations either keep those things alive or delete them. There is no more human sacrifice, transport by horse and cart, rickety old cars, or messages via telegram as a way of life.

God and religion and afterlife are as real as each other based upon the insights and revelations of holy men. The Old World Order which we have moved away from. The world of cultural horrors (like all historic wars) or superstitions, but they were innocent to the potentials of today's obliteration via atomic bombs, climate change, pandemics, biological weapons, and pollution. I add loss of the soul to that list without evidence only strong belief.

The Soviet Union detonated a nuclear bomb over 1500 hundred times more powerful than the US one dropped on Hiroshima and Nagasaki combined! Drop enough of them billions die is the thought here.

More likely a threat is another Covid-19 type disease.

H5N1 / Bird flu is one of the greatest threats the human race because if it jumps from birds to humans the death rate is very high whereas for Covid-19 it is very low.

Basically; pandemics are human caused. The reason is deforestation for road, town building, or for crop space. Which means humans are passing near the contagious animals that were once hidden away far away in jungles or forests. And then animals not normally associated to coming into contact with humans can via blood or other reasons of contact, like eating them, cause a jump of a deadly virus to humans.

More ecological variety has increased advantages for viruses to jump into another species rather than humans. It is predicted as we expand further into forest territories there will more pandemics. Welcome to death.

Chapter 9

Calculation Collective

So that is just how the world is. It supports nearly 8 billion but alas we do not have the money and systems in place to aid the victims of that system. Pollution gets worse not better as seen in oceans filling with plastic, CO2 emissions in the air and vehicle emissions.

It is a great opportunity to create power togetherness and confrontation to those we deem greedy. The main causes of this are business political greed machines. The UN and EU have not policed them well enough.

The future of the Human race will come to exist – on our collective calculation, or lack of it, and use of our reflective soul powers. Once done this climate change becomes a lot clearer and fairer for people. Then we can win it. Then we can alter things. As it is a few very dangerous greedy groups dictate change, via business, finance, political, media manipulation, and articulate fixed laws written by intelligent bright university educated people that suit those organizations and their natural methods to change the world.

As it is, it is a misguiding con of the lowest ever order. Politicians, business tax cheating elites, media moguls and banking systems of colossal debt, they need a head on collision: with people. Such a collision is like producing a calculation. And it is this calculation that is missing within society.

Politics, banks, media and business actually run a calculation system between them that favours them. This plays out naturally and has no real way of stopping it via political influences because politics lets it run into what is a complex unpredictable system where information is churning out across the planet at such a quick speed it takes 40 years to decide we need to tackle climate change, and a similar time to realize we run all countries on mountains of debt and armies with atom bombs, and media companies that cannot grasp the truth that they can present to people and to which people might listen.

Business is the order of the day and business is run to fleece the environment and has tipped environmental reality into a climate crisis and slow consistent deleting of species that is going to play out whilst being accompanied by fires, floods, and lost crops.

The biggest deceit? All ideas of hope it will end well. It is virtually impossible it will end in sweet dreams – we do not have the systems or even the money dynamics to achieve the hopeful tasks. The system is created over decades. 4 year government plans do not solve much and are pretty much in keeping with extending the current system of increasing debt, increasing production, increasing arms. Not switching to green energy quickly enough. The very idea goes against the very thought process and structure that thought process built.

Governments lack coherency with business activity to deactivate coal use, which in turn connects to jobs and payment for rents and food. These connections of links are not easily enough altered because of reliance to money structures and deployment of resources. It is like saying if we all diet and run five miles a day we will all be fit. Yes, it is possible but humans do not act to the best purposes. We connect to the habits we endorse. And so for our fitness and food habits, so too for politics and business dynamics. Hence the New World Destructive Order will continue. It is a mistake to say IT will change in time. That is part of its illusion – all will be fine. IT is hidden in time information dimensions where IT wears down all counter measures over time. So it is the information energy complex is baked into the New World Destructive Order. And so it is as you read this you can certain you too carry a mind-set that in part is naturally structured with some of ITs mechanics. Why? Because you watch media, use the internet, because you buy from businesses and play a part in working for a business, you vote and accept politicians. And you as an individual have absolutely no idea whatsoever what your innocent contribution is to its fabric of existence. Just as you don't know how much you contribute to the constructive order where you will be a part of maintaining love, care, respect for life, and emotions like joy, ethical intelligence and sustaining of the biological order and spiritual order.

Individuals understand time because of clocks. But here with the New World Destructive Order we have no invention to aid us. And you must face the judgement of your maker, or if Buddhist the karma of your ways. However, what is certain, sister, is that looked at on the collective scale in relation to climate change we can be certain a biological attack is occurring made via CO2 emissions that wipe out species and hold a potential to wipe out civilization as we know it. Carry on as we are and we play Russian roulette with our soul our meaning to life and connection to God – that is my message to you, sister.

Climate change actually shows us we are going wrong and our choice now is to try and put it right. If we do not try, as well we should, then that is our virtue as a collective not a judgement of any individual. I have merely pointed out that the main tenets of this destructive cause are politicians and business and media, all held in place by university educated people with big expensive ambitions where the side effect is climate change. And where it was known about decades ago and not responded to quickly enough because of a collective mind set which under no circumstances involves the calculation of uneducated people. Far from it, it is the calculation of university people, or rather the lack of care to calculate carefully enough.

And all they will say out loud when they read this, these educated custodians of society – We built society we did a lot of good.

Yes, I agree, but the side effect to those goods is climate change and the side effect to business pollution and political acceptance is climate change. And the side effects of the media not educating us and reporting enough on climate change means we sit back and let climate change continue. Where at a certain point we not only wipe out most species and most humans but we wipe out our very morality that we believe in and which reflects our spiritual nature towards a creator: God. What was the point in having a worldwide university system, if that is to be the side effect? Such is my message to you, sister.

Chapter 10

Bye, Bye, not Buy Buy!

So that is the end of part one of what is 3 books. I could have put them into one book but the content is challenging and leaves much to reflect over. I certainly do not assume any academic, politician, business person, or media worker to be anything less than any other individual. But as a group and what emerges from them as a collective is without doubt one of the most dangerous strains of the New World Destructive Order.

So what next? Well, you might ask why someone would write a message to two groups of religious women and it not be explained why. I mean logically you might have read all this and concluded it is open to anyone. You will find out sure enough why I am so specific, one reason (but not the main reason) is that the two religious books you favour use the term Satan and although this can be very misleading it is actually quite informative in what is a basic framed insight.

I have not harped on into detail as to what else could define such a word but in the modern day intellectual standing such a word would be viewed in a contemptuous light as if no thought should be put to it. Whereas a reader of your two holy books sees that there is reference.

And so you should then ask – then why is it not called Message for the Brothers and Sisters? I wish it was but so it stands… and next we meet I will offer you a very interesting choice. If you don't like choices then keep away, but let us not forget wisdom – curiosity killed the cat! Let us hope it does not kill the sisters. I can assure you that is not the intention. It may well make the sisters.

So whoever you are reading this – good luck, or as better said with no luck involved: God Bless you.

End of part one part.

CHACHA CHAUDHARY AND TOILET

WOW! WHAT A NICE IDEA. CAN'T WE ALSO DO IT, CHACHA JI?
NO ! BECAUSE A MUG AND BUCKET INDICATES THAT THEY ARE GOING FOR DEFECATION AND NOT A MORNING WALK.
FOR DEFECATION ! THAT TOO IN OPEN!
YES !
THIS IS NOT A RIGHT THING TO DO.
I AGREE ! IT'S REALLY NOT CORRECT.
AND WE HAVE TO MAKE THEM UNDERSTAND THIS.

STOP ! STOP ! WHY ARE YOU ALL RUNNING?
OH ! DON'T STOP US. IT'S STINKING HERE.

AH ! WE CAN'T TOLERATE IT.
WAIT! WAIT! SPEND SOME TIME IN THIS FOUL SMELL IT'S CREATED BY ALL OF YOU ONLY.

WHAT DO YOU MEAN ?
IT MEANS.... THIS DIRTY SMELL IS ALL BECAUSE OF OPEN DEFECATION BY ALL OF YOU VILLAGERS.

NOT JUST THE SMELL THIS DIRT WOULD ALSO CAUSE A LOT OF DISEASES.
HOW ?

IF YOU DEFECATE IN OPEN FLIES WILL SIT ON IT AND SPREAD THE GERMS AROUND...
THE FLIES WILL THEN SIT ON THE FOOD, WATER, AND CONTAMINATE IT, WHICH WILL MAKE ALL OF YOU SICK.

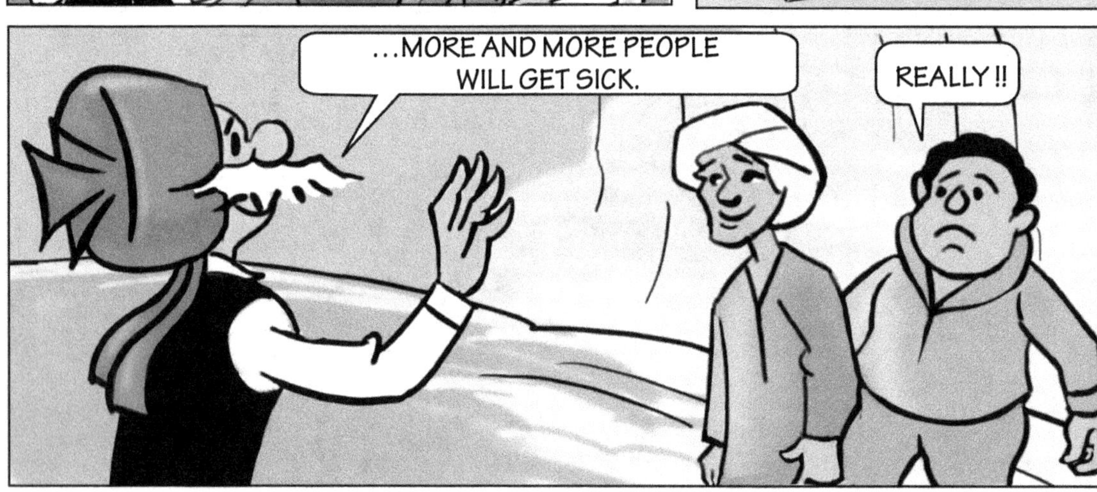

...MORE AND MORE PEOPLE WILL GET SICK.
REALLY !!

BUT CHACHA JI, HOW CAN WE PREVENT IT? DEFECATION IS VERY IMPORTANT
TRUE ! BUT YOU CAN AVOID GOING IN THE OPEN.

FOR THIS, WE NEED TO CONSTRUCT TOILETS IN OUR HOMES.

BY BUILDING TOILETS IN OUR HOMES, THE WHOLE ENVIRONMENT WILL BE CLEAN AND BEAUTIFUL...

... AND YOU WILL BE SAVED FROM UNWANTED DISEASES.
HOSPITAL

ALSO, THE FEMALE MEMBERS OF YOUR FAMILY WILL NOT HAVE TO FACE THE HUMILIATION OF DEFECATING IN OPEN.

YOU ARE RIGHT, CHACHA JI. BUT WE CAN'T AFFORD TO BUILD TOILETS IN OUR HOMES. IT COSTS TOO MUCH.

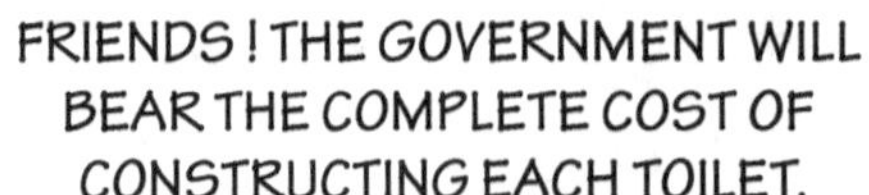

FRIENDS ! THE GOVERNMENT WILL BEAR THE COMPLETE COST OF CONSTRUCTING EACH TOILET.

OUR GOVT. HAS TAKEN THE RESPONSIBILITY TO CONSTRUCT TOILET IN THE RURAL AREAS, BEING FUNDED BY "PRADHAN MANTRI SWACHHTA KOSH."

OUR GOVERNMENT IS COMMITTED TO CONSTRUCT TOILET IN EACH AND EVERY VILLAGE AND IT'S ONLY POSSIBLE…

WHEN WE ALL SAY TOGETHER…

WE PLEDGE TO HAVE A TOILET IN OUR HOUSE.
GOOD ! IF YOU WANT YOUR WIFE TO BE HAPPY, THEN A TOILET IN HOME IS A NECESSITY.

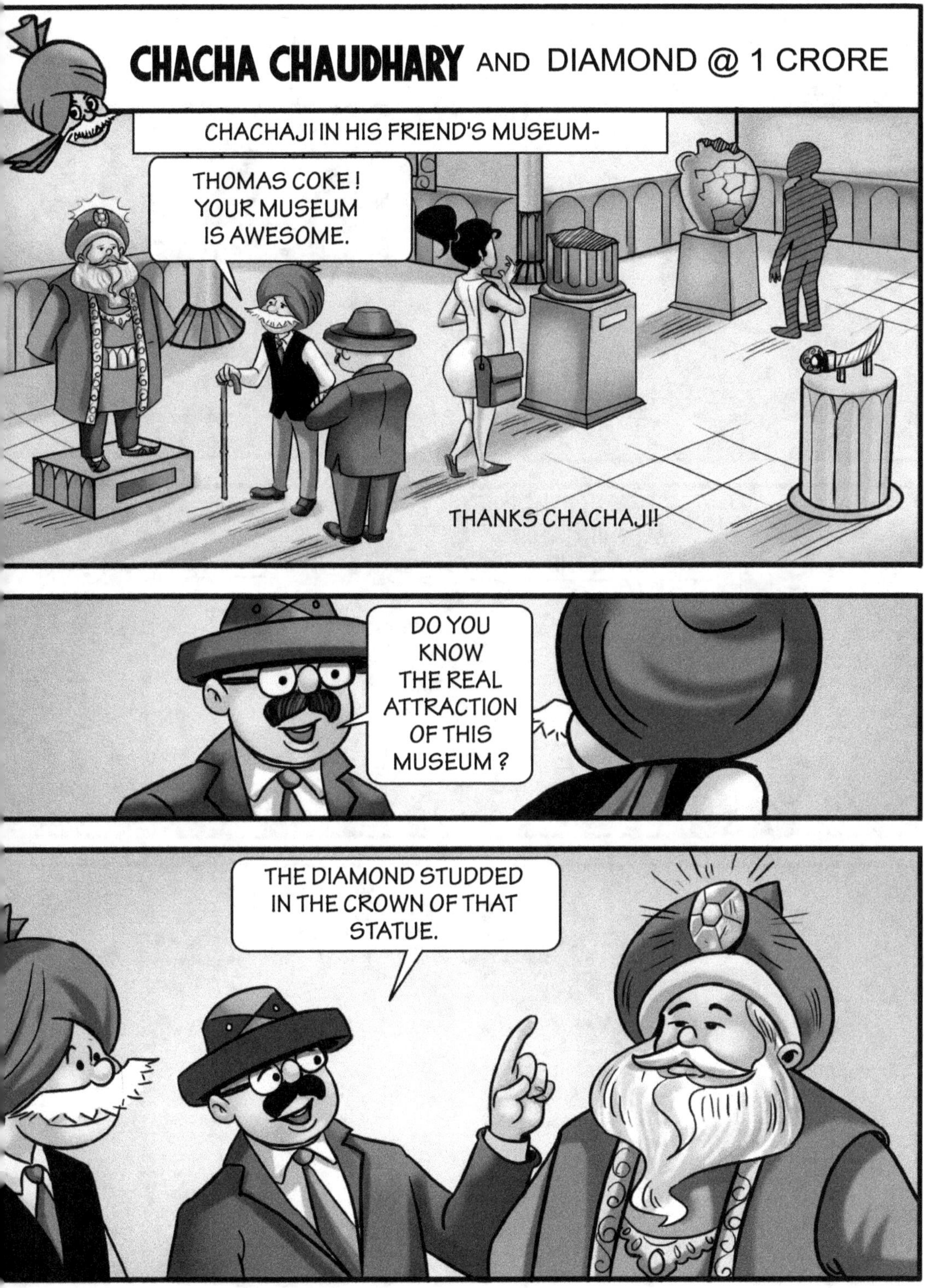

CHACHA CHAUDHARY AND DIAMOND @ 1 CRORE

REALLY !!

IT IS WORTH RS 1 CRORE.

IT WAS A PLEASURE WATCHING THIS DIAMOND.

I'LL TAKE YOUR LEAVE NOW.
© PRAN'S FEATURES

www.chachachaudhary.com

THE THIEF MUST BE A PERSON CLOSE TO YOU.

PLEASE FIND IT QUICKLY CHACHAJI! OTHERWISE IT WILL BE TAKEN OUT OF THE COUNTRY.

I'LL HAVE TO DO SOMETHING FAST.

CHACHA CHAUDHARY'S BRAIN WORKS FASTER THAN COMPUTER.

IN THE MEANTIME-

HA-HA!! MR GLASCO, I TOOK RS 1 CRORE ADVANCE FROM YOU... AND I'VE DONE YOUR JOB.

THE DIAMOND IS WITH ME.

HERE IS THE DIAMOND.

THIS DIAMOND ISN'T WORTH RS. 100 ALSO.
OH!

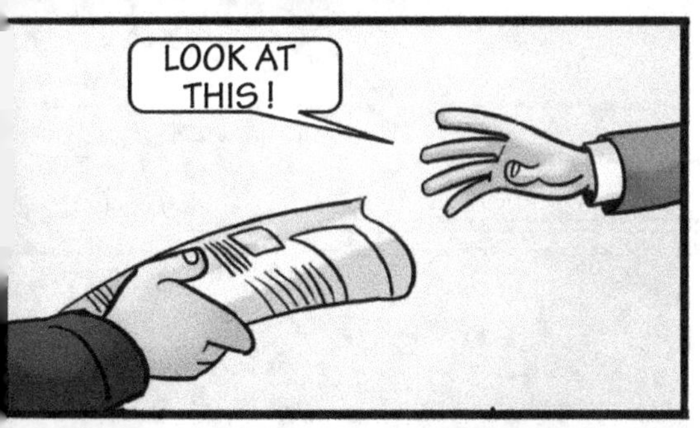

LOOK AT THIS!

!!

THE THIEF HAS STOLEN A FAKE DIAMOND FROM THE MUSEUM. THE DIAMOND WORTH 1 CRORE IS STILL SAFE.

IT'S CHEATING.

YOU ARE CHEATING ME.

BRING ME THE ORIGINAL DIAMOND OR GET MY MONEY BACK.
I'LL GET THE ORIGINAL DIAMOND FOR YOU.

IT ISN'T DIFFICULT FOR ME TO STEAL IN THE MUSEUM AGAIN.

THAT NIGHT.
I HAVE ALL THE DUPLICATE KEYS OF THE MUSEUM.

I AM INSIDE NOW.

THERE'S A DIAMOND IN THE STATUE'S CROWN.

THIS IS THE ORIGINAL DIAMOND.

THIS DIAMOND IS FAKE.
YOU'LL TELL WHERE THE REAL DIAMOND IS.

OH! THE STATUE'S SPEAKING

13

THIS STATUE NOT ONLY SPEAKS BUT ALSO BEATS.
BANG !!
OH !! CHACHA CHAUDHARY !!
YES, I HAD TO BECOME A STATUE TO CATCH THE DIAMOND THIEF. BECAUSE ...

... I GOT THE NEWS PRINTED IN THE NEWSPAPER THAT THE STOLEN DIAMOND IS FAKE.
YOU WON'T SURVIVE.
STOP IT.
BOOM!!

SO YOU'RE CAUGHT.
YOU PEST!

HERE'S YOUR DIAMOND THIEF. NOW HE'LL TELL THE WHEREABOUTS OF THE ORIGINAL DIAMOND.
HE'S MY SON.

I SECRETLY GOT THE DUPLICATE OF ALL THE KEYS MADE.

I WAS BLINDED WITH THE GLIMMER OF 1 CRORE RS. SO I STOLE THE DIAMOND.

OUR SCRIPTURES ARE SO TRUE, AN INSIDER CAN CAUSE US MAXIMUM HARM.

16

CHACHA CHAUDHARY AND STOMACHFUL MEAL

www.chachachaudhary.com

GREETINGS CHACHAJI !!
COME PAKDU LAL !
© PRAN'S FEATURES
HOW CAN I HELP YOU ?
I'VE COME TO GET A SOLUTION.
TELL ME OF A TRICK TO SAVE MYSELF FROM MY WIFE.
I CAN SAVE YOU FROM ANY TROUBLE IN THIS WORLD, BUT I DON'T HAVE ANY SOLUTION FOR THIS PROBLEM.
IF I HAD A SOLUTION, I WOULD HAVE USED IT TO SAVE MYSELF FROM YOUR CHACHI.

CHACHAJI! CHACHI!
GRRR!!

I'M GONE.
GRRR! YOU TALK LIKE THIS ABOUT ME???

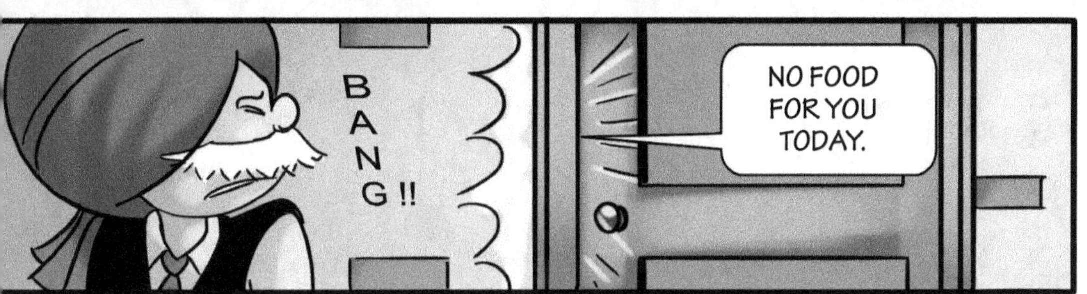

B A N G!!
NO FOOD FOR YOU TODAY.

THIS PAKDU LAL HAS CREATED PROBLEM IN MY HOUSE.
WHERE'S HE GONE??
HE ESCAPED EARLIER ONLY.

COME ! LET'S GO OUT AND ARRANGE FOR SOMETHING TO EAT.

IN THE MEANTIME, NEARBY...
BABA'S FOOD JOINT
BABA'S FOOD JOINT - STOMACH FUL MEAL IN RS. 50.

IT'S A WONDERFUL OFFER.

ONE DOES NOT GET MUCH INRS 50 NOWADAYS.

THEN WHY THE DELAY ? LET'S GO AND HAVE A STOMACH FULL MEAL.
TAKE THE TOKEN FIRST.

EVERYBODY OF THE TEMPLE REMAIN CLOSED.

EVERY ONE SIT ON A CHAIR TO EAT IN A DHABA.

DHABA OWNER BABA !

HAVE IT ! ENJOY !!
HOW CAN WE EAT CHAPATI ALONE ? BRING SOME VEGETABLE ALSO.

RS. 100 FOR A VEGETABLE.

21

THE ONES WHO WON'T TAKE A VEGETABLE.
...WILL HAVE TO EAT CHAPATI ONLY.

PAY EXTRA FOR THE VEGETABLES.

THIS IS CHEATING. IT'S WRITTEN ON THE BOARD OUTSIDE STOMACH FULL MEAL IN RS. 50.
BABA'S FOOD JOINT - STOMACH FUL MEAL IN RS. 50.

THAT'S ONLY FOR THE CHAPATI. NOT THE VEGETABLE. UNDERSTAND ??

HERE'S THE MONEY FOR THE VEGETABLE.
100

GIVE ME ALSO.
ME TOO.
HA-HA-HA!
SOB! SOB! WE'RE CHEATED.
WHAT HAPPENED? WHY IS EVERYONE SO SAD?
COME SABU! LET'S GO TO THIS FOOD JOINT.
THIS IS CHEATING.

YOU'VE OPENED A VERY REASONABLE FOOD JOINT.

CAN YOU FEED STOMACH FULL MEAL TO MY FRIEND IN RS. 50 ?
YES ! YES !!

TAKE RS. 50.
50

CALL YOUR FRIEND.

COME SABU.

BRING THE CHAPATIS.

IS THE VEGETABLE REQUIRED ?
MY FRIEND DOESN'T EAT VEGETABLES. HE EATS ONLY CHAPATIS. JUST FEED HIM STOMACH FULL OF THAT.

BRING MORE CHAPATIS.

BRING MORE.

BRING MORE.

BRING !!

BRING.

25

ALL CHAPATIS
ARE
FINISHED.

150 KG FLOUR IS FINISHED

4 GAS
CYLINDERS
ARE
FINISHED.

I AM STILL HUNGRY.
CRASH !

YOU
PROMISED
TO GIVE
STOMACH
FULL MEAL.
PLEASE
SPARE US !

RETURN THE
MONEY OF
ALL
THOSE WHOM
YOU CHEATED.

... NOW LEAVE
THIS CITY.
RUN !!
HA-HA-HA !!

PRAN'S
CHACHA CHAUDHARY
AND
ROCK BAND
STADIUM

SUNNY WITH TWITTER AND GOOGLE.
CHACHA CHAUDHARY AND ROCK BAND
SUMMER HOLIDAYS HAVE BEGUN. WHAT'S THE PLAN FOR HOLIDAYS.
NOT DECIDED YET.
MUST HAVE THOUGHT OF SOME THING.

NEWSPAPER!

HERE'S THE PLAN!
BEEGEES ROCK BAND PERFORM IN CITY.

WOW ! BEEGEES ROCK BAND SHOW IN OUR TOWN.
WE'LL DEFINITELY SEE THIS SHOW.
I'LL BOOK THE TICKETS ONLINE.

I'LL TAKE BEEGEES AUTOGRAPH ON MY T-SHIRT.
STA

THE SHOW WILL BE IN THIS STADIUM.
STADIUM
IT'S CROWDED.

I CAN SMELL SOMETHING PECULIAR SMELL.

IT'S OF THOSE RATS.
WHAT ARE THEY DOING.

29

THEY ARE ROAMING AROUND THAT MYSTERIOUS MAN. SOMETHING IS WRONG. I MUST INFORM CHACHA CHAUDHARY.
I'LL JUST COME!
SOON.
WE MUST STOP HIM.
AS YOU HAVE DESCRIBED, THE MATTER IS SERIOUS. SOMETHING CAN GO WRONG.
BEEGEES ARE PERFORMING ON THE STAGE, NOTHING HAS HAPPENED YET.
LET'S GO INSIDE.
SABU! YOU STAY IN FRONT OF THE STADIUM AND KEEP AN EYE ON PEOPLE COMING.

SUDDENLY.
CHACHA JI! SAME SMELL. THOSE RATS AND THE PERSON MUST BE NEARBY.
CAN'T FIND THEM IN THE CROWD. WE MUST BE ALERT.
THE TROUBLE WAS SOME WHERE ELSE.
WELL DONE! CUT THE STAG SO THAT IT FALLS ON BEEGEES, AND THEY'LL NEVER PERFORM AGAIN.
IT'S DONE! THE STAG WILL FALL ON BEEGEES.
THE STAG IS GOING TO FALL ON BEEGEES, CHACHA JI!
NOTHING WILL HAPPEN TO BEEGEES.
A PORTION OF THE STAG IS GOING TO FALL ON THE BEEGEES.

THE STAGE FALLS ON THE FLOOR.
THUD D !!

CHACHA CHAUDHARY HAS UPSET MY PLAN.

I MUST ESCAPE.
SUNNY RUNS AFTER THE VILLAIN.

SABU ! CATCH HIM.

WHERE WILL YOU GO ?

OHH !
TO JAIL !

THANKS !
CHACHA JI. YOU
SAVED ME FROM
MY ENEMY.

YOUR LIFE WAS
SAVED DUE TO
SUNNY'S ALERTNESS.
HE'S YOURZ BIG FAN.

I NEED YOUR
AUTOGRAPH,
NOT THANK YOU.
WE ALSO.

TODAY IT'LL BE
OPPOSITE. I'LL TAKE
YOUR AUTOGRAPH.
YOU SAVED MY LIFE.

HA ! HA !!

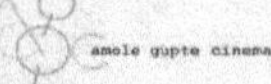

Eros International presents
A Trinity Pictures Franchise of an Amole Gupte Cinema production
EROS
"Sniff!!!"
SPY
a Film by amole gupte
DANGER KI SMELL KYA HOTI HAI?
RELEASING
25TH AUGUST

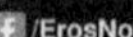

EROS
techzone
www.erosnow.com   /ErosNow   @ErosNow   @Eros_Now   /ErosNow
EROSNOW
AN EROS INTERNATIONAL WORLDWIDE RELEASE

CHACHA CHAUDHARY
CHAMPION

JUMP!!

SKI DIVING SPORTS PRACTICE.

SKI DIVERS ARE SHOWING GOOD TRICKS.

GROUND IS COMING NEARER.
© PRAN'S FEATURES

ROCKY! YOU'RE NOT OPENING THE PARACHUTE?
LUKA! YOU OPEN FIRST.
YOU CAN'T TRY TO COMPETE WITH ME.

35

I'VE OPENED THE PARACHUTE.
I'VE ALSO.

ROCKY! IT WAS A GOOD LANDING.

NEXT TIME I'LL STAY FOR A LONGER TIME WITHOUT THE PARACHUTE.

THIS TIME I WANT TO BECOME THE CHAMPION SKI DIVER.
LUKA! YOU BETTER FORGET THIS DREAM.

BY HOOK OR BY CROOK I'VE TO BECOME THE CHAMPION.
WE'LL HAVE TO TAMPER WITH ROCKY'S PARACHUTE.

THE SKI DIVING CHAMPIONSHIP TAKES PLACE AFTER TEA BREAK.

ROCKY'S PARACHUTE IS TIED IN SUCH A WAY THAT IT WON'T OPEN IN THE SKY.

BEST OF LUCK !

SWISH !!
www.chachachaudhary.com

ROCKY ! LUKA ! JUMP !

I'M GOING TO OPEN THE PARACHUTE.
I'LL REMAIN IN THE SKY FOR A LONGER TIME TO WIN THE CHAMPIONSHIP.

THE COMPETITION IS INTERESTING
ROCKY IS TAKING A RISK TO WIN.

NOW GROUND IS NEAR. I SHOULD OPEN THE PARACHUTE.

OH !! IT'S NOT OPENING.

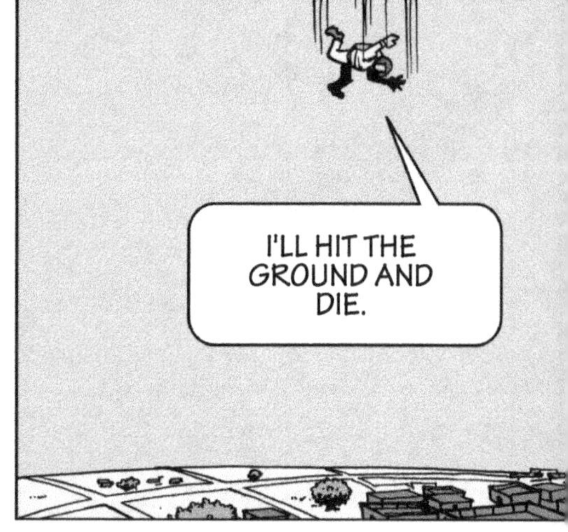

I'LL HIT THE GROUND AND DIE.

38

HO ! HO !!
YOU'LL DIE
AND I'LL
BE THE
CHAMPION.
THIS IS
YOUR
TRICK.

SABU !
SAVE
ROCKY !

HU-
HUBA !
THANK
GOD !
I COULD
HOLD YOU !

YOU'RE
THE REAL
CHAMPION.

YOU'LL BE
IMPRISONED IN
THE ATTEMPT TO
KILL ROCKY.

CHACHA CHAUDHARY
AND
BANK ROBBERS

CASH
PUT ALL THE CASH IN MY BAG, ELSE...

CATCH THEM! THEY'VE LOOTED A BANK.
www.chachachaudhary.com

CHACHA CHAUDHARY! CITY BANK HAS BEEN ROBBED!

DON'T WORRY! THE CULPRITS CAN'T ESCAPE.

LADO! WE'LL CROSS THE TOLL AND ENTER THE OTHER CITY.
WOW!

WHY DID YOU STOP THE CAR?
THE ROAD IS CLOSED AHEAD.

THAT RED TURBAN HAS BLOCKED THE WAY.
CHACHA CHAUDHARY?
HE'S MORE DANGEROUS THAN THE POLICE.

BANK ROBBERS COME OUT OF YOUR CAR AND SURRENDER.

GRRR!
TAKE THE REVERSE GEAR AND RUN FROM HERE.

OH ! CHACHA AND SABU BOTH !
THUD !!

YOU WON'T AGREE EASILY ?

HU-HUBA !

PUT US DOWN !

SABU ! DROP THEM AT THE POLICE STATION.
© PRAN'S FEATURES

42

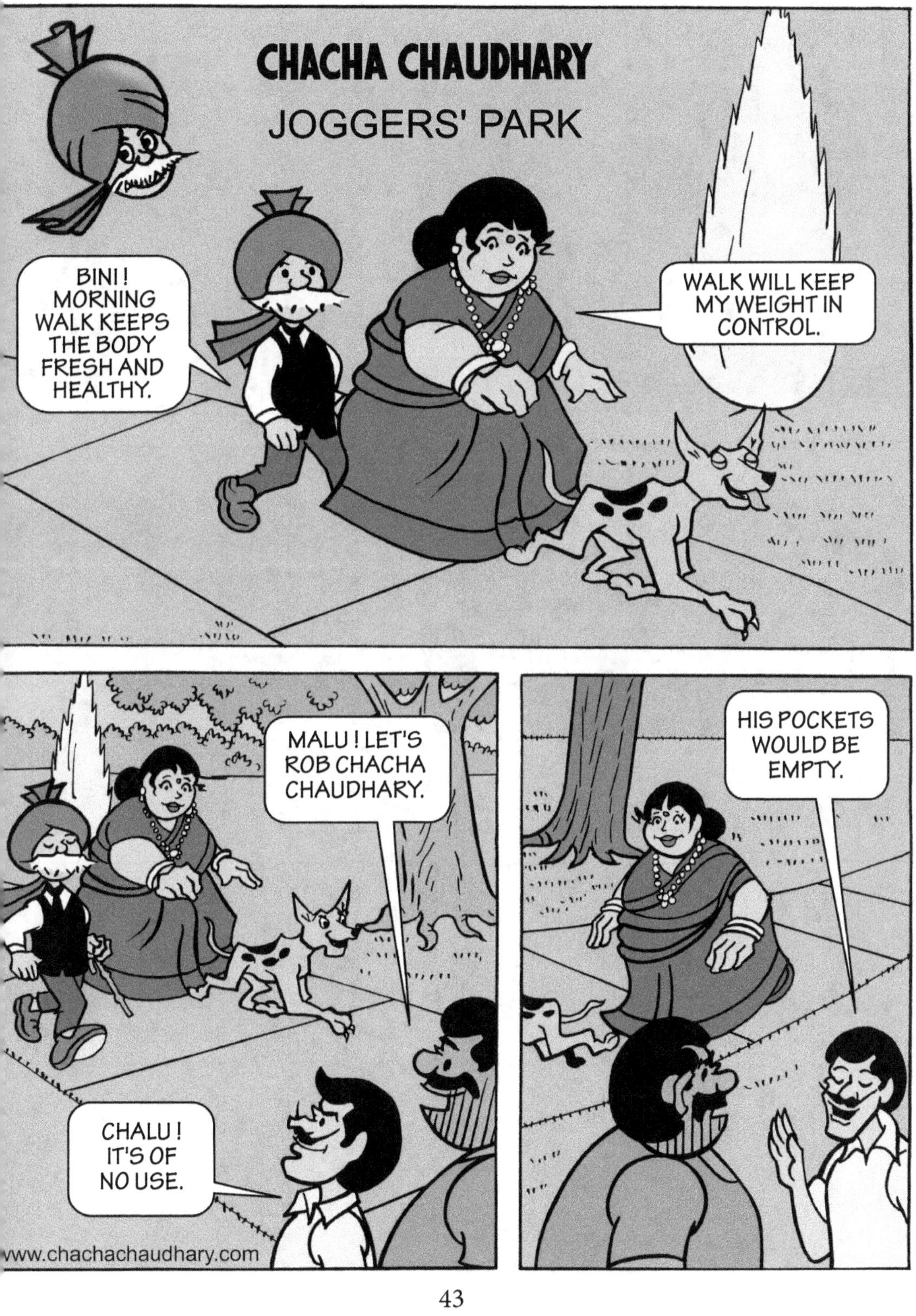

CHACHA CHAUDHARY

JOGGERS' PARK

HIS WIFE IS WEARING EXPENSIVE ORNAMENTS.
WE CAN SNATCH THAT.

HAND ALL THE JEWELLERY TO US.

GRRR !!

BOW!!! WOW!!
OH !
© PRAN'S FEATURES

GIVE MILK TO THAT DOG TO KEEP HIM BUSY.

THICK, CREAMY MILK FOR YOU.

TILL THE TIME HE IS DRINKING, WE CAN ROB THAT LADY.

NOW GIVE ALL THESE ORNAMENTS TO ME.

THE ORNAMENTS ARE FAKE. THE GOLD WATCH IS ORIGINAL.

CHAUDHARY! GIVE ME THE WATCH OR YOU'LL BE KILLED.

GO, YOU'RE SAVED.

I'LL SELL THIS WATCH AND COME.

SOME DISTANCE.
YOU TRAM! RETURN CHACHAJI'S WATCH.

IT'S MY WATCH.
THERE IS A TRANSMITTER IN THAT WATCH.

ITS SIGNAL COMES IN THIS WALKY-TALKY.

COME WITH ME TO THE PRISON.

CHACHA CHAUDHARY
COCONUT

SABU ! I'VE TO MAKE A WINDOW IN THAT WALL. YOU MAKE A HOLE IN THAT WALL AND MY JOB WILL BE EASIER.

I'LL HIT MY HEAD THERE.

THUD !!
HU-HUBA !

WOW ! NOW I'LL PUT THE WOODEN FRAME AND FIT THE WINDOW.
SABU'S HEAD WILL BE OF USE TO ME ALSO.
www.chachachaudhary.com

47

YOUR HEAD IS SO POWERFUL AND STRONG.
SO ??

HIT IT AGAINST A COCONUT.

OK !

THUD !!!

OH ! IT'S SMASHED.
© PRAN'S FEATURES

9 789352 784172